Americans All biographies are inspiring life stories about people of all races, creeds, and nationalities who have uniquely contributed to the American way of life. Highlights from each person's story develop his contributions in his special field — whether they be in the arts, industry, human rights, education, science and medicine, or sports.

Specific abilities, character, and accomplishments are emphasized. Often despite great odds, these famous people have attained success in their fields through the good use of ability, determination, and hard work. These fast-moving stories of real people will show the way to better understanding of the ingredients necessary for personal success.

Will Rogers

COWBOY PHILOSOPHER

by Elizabeth Rider Montgomery

illustrated by Victor Mays

GARRARD PUBLISHING COMPANY
CHAMPAIGN, ILLINOIS

For Douglas Small

Picture credits:

Brown Brothers: p. 16, 57, 64, 67, 74, 80, 87 (both)
Museum of Modern Art: p. 2
Wide World: p. 31

Standard Book Number: 8116-4562-2

Library of Congress Catalog Card Number: 79-115469

Contents

1. "Born Bowlegged"

Will Rogers raced his little chestnut mare into his sister's farmyard. Screaming at the top of his lungs, he whirled his lasso around his head and sent it sailing through the air. As the lasso landed neatly around the gatepost, Will gave a final high-pitched shout and brought his pony up short.

"I'm home!" he shrieked joyfully.

Will's sister Sallie and her husband, Tom McSpadden, appeared in the farmhouse doorway. They tried to look stern, but neither could keep from smiling at the happy-go-lucky eight-year-old.

It was the year 1887. The Rogers and McSpadden families lived in Indian Territory, which included most of the present state of Oklahoma. Since there was no school close to Will's own home near Oologah, he was living with his married sister Sallie. He attended a one-room Cherokee school.

The Cherokee Indians were noted for their peaceful and progressive ways. Both of Will Rogers' parents were one-fourth Cherokee, and they were very proud of it.

Will, who loved to ride, traveled to and from school on his pony. As Territory folks said, "He was born bowlegged so he could sit a horse."

"I'm home!" Will repeated now, jumping off his pony.

"So we see, Willie," said his brother-in-law.

"And hear," Sallie added. "I reckon you're about the noisiest little boy in Indian Territory, Willie Rogers."

"Also the laziest," Tom put in. "But that's going to change right now. As soon as you take care of your pony, Willie, come to the barn. I'm going to teach you how to milk."

Will's eyes opened wide in horror. Milk cows? That would be *work*!

"Good land, Tom," Will protested. "I can't. I . . . I've got a lame knee."

"It didn't seem to bother you in riding," Tom remarked dryly.

"But with milking, it's different," Will explained earnestly. "In milking I'd have to stoop, like this." He pretended to sit on a milking stool. Then he screwed up his

9

eyes as if in pain and let out an ear-splitting shriek. "Ow!"

Sallie and Tom laughed. Willie was such a lovable little clown!

Will was the eighth child in the Clem Rogers family. Four of the Rogers children had died, and Will was the only surviving boy. His fun-loving mother, his three much-older sisters, and even his serious, businesslike father spoiled him badly.

Clem Rogers, whom everybody called "Uncle Clem," was a cattle rancher, a banker, and a leader in the affairs of the Cherokee Nation. He gave his children nearly everything they wanted. Going to school was the only thing Willie Rogers had ever done that he didn't want to do.

Coiling his lasso neatly, Will asked his sister, "Will you play the organ after supper, Sallie?"

Sallie agreed. "Yes, Willie, and we'll all sing."

Will loved to sing. It reminded him of his home and his mother. He often sang with her while she played their piano—the only one in the neighborhood.

Will didn't accomplish much at school, except to become known among his Cherokee classmates as a champion roper and rider. In the races and contests held during noon hours, Will usually won.

He also excelled in passing the water bucket. The boys took turns carrying the water bucket to the spring, filling it, and then passing it around to the thirty thirsty pupils sitting on split log benches. When it was Will's turn to pass the bucket, he could spill more water and make more classmates laugh than any other boy.

When the school year ended, Clem Rogers decided to send Will to the Cherokee seminary, where his sisters May and Maude were students. But Will did not study there, either. He spent most of his time roping, clowning, and playing tricks on his classmates.

When Will was ten years old his mother died. Her death was a terrible blow to him. Will and his mother had been very close, and Clem Rogers did not understand his harum-scarum son.

2. Cadet Show-off

Uncle Clem enrolled his son in another school, then another, and another, but Willie simply would not study.

"There's a lot of mule in Willie," Clem Rogers sighed.

In January, 1897, Clem took seventeen-year-old Will to Kemper Military School in Boonville, Missouri. Straight and trim in their military uniforms, the cadets stared at the new boy. Will wore a cowboy hat with a long horsehair cord around it, a brilliant shirt, an equally flashy vest,

and his pants tucked into cowboy boots. Around his neck was a flame-red bandanna. His trunk was tied with a lasso.

Will appeared to ignore his wide-eyed audience, but he swaggered more than usual in order to cover his uneasiness at the sight of so many strange faces.

"Good-bye, Son," said Uncle Clem. "Work hard, now."

"Good-bye, Papa," Will drawled, trying to act indifferent about the parting.

Uncle Clem left, hoping that the strict routine and the rigid discipline would encourage his son to start studying.

Will, however, had no intention of studying. He had a remarkable memory, and he used it to get by without working.

"Tell me what today's lesson is about, Hurt," Will would ask his friend as they hurried down the hall to a class.

Hurt was glad to oblige. He liked Will, even though his roommate was fond of playing pranks like tipping over his bunk and dumping him out on the floor. Besides, Hurt liked to show off how well he had studied.

In class if a teacher asked Will a question he couldn't answer, he would ask one in return. That usually started an argument, and by the time it was settled, the

Will as a cadet at Kemper Military School

teacher had forgotten what the original question was.

If he couldn't evade answering a question, Will made the class laugh. Sometimes he did it by cocking an eyebrow, rubbing his chin, or scratching his head. Sometimes he did it with a witty remark. The students at Kemper Military School liked Will Rogers, and the other cadets often repeated the funny things he said.

The first time Will went home from Kemper for a holiday, he enjoyed telling the Oologah boys about military school. He made everything sound better and more exciting than it really was.

"It's just like being in the army," Will boasted, although he actually hated the strict routine. "We get up at bugle call and go to bed at bugle call. We have rifle drills and we do guard duty in a brick courtyard. Every time we get caught breaking the rules, we get extra guard duty." Will grinned. "I've marched up and down that courtyard so often you can see my footprints in every brick."

"Do you have a real gun for drilling?" asked one of his friends.

"Sure. I'll show you." Will went into the house and got his father's rifle. Then he demonstrated Kemper's rifle drill, performing each move with precision. When it was time to lower the gun to the ground, he struck the butt against the earth so hard that the gun went off with a roar. The bullet grazed Will's forehead, and his hat flew off.

The other boys scampered away, afraid they would be blamed for the accident, but Will stood still, blood dripping down his face.

"What happened?" roared Uncle Clem from the doorway.

Will's narrow escape had left him speechless. He couldn't think of an excuse or a joke. He simply walked to his father and handed him the gun. Will Rogers never again touched a gun voluntarily.

Back at Kemper after the holidays, Will developed a routine for roping practice. He offered twenty-five cents an hour to every boy who would let himself be roped.

Will sorted out the volunteers according to size. To the little boys he said, "You'll be the calves, and I'll rope you around the left leg. Stoop over now, and run and bawl like calves."

The little boys set out on all fours, and Will roped each one by the left leg.

Then he started with the middle-sized cadets. "You're the cows," he said. "I'll rope you around your right legs." And he did just that.

"Now," said Will to the others, "you big fellows are steers. I'll rope each of you around the middle."

The boys often suffered bruises and rope burns during Will's roping practice. Some-

times they were even dragged over the ground on their backs or their heads. No one minded, however, because it was fun, and it was also pleasant to get twenty-five cents an hour. Besides, Will usually provided a treat for his "calves, cows, and steers" when the practice hour ended.

"Come on downtown, fellows," he would say, unless his father's generous check had already melted away. "I'll treat you."

Downtown the boys would sit on round-topped stools at a counter and eat chili, Will's favorite food.

After little more than a year at Kemper, Will decided he had had enough schooling. He wrote to his three sisters, who were all married now, telling them he needed money badly. Each one sent him ten dollars. Will packed a suitcase, tied it with his lasso, and ran away from Kemper. He left about 150 hours of accumulated guard duty.

"That's one debt I'll never have to pay," he said gleefully.

3. Indian Cowboy

Will, now eighteen, had no intention of going home. He knew that Uncle Clem would lecture him and perhaps insist that he go back to school. A Kemper cadet had told him about a friend's cattle ranch near Higgins, Texas, so Will decided to go there.

"I'm Will Rogers, from Indian Territory," he told the ranch owner. "I'd like a job. I'm a good worker." Will was sure he would be a good worker when he found an occupation that interested him.

Mr. Ewing, the rancher, studied the slender, wiry figure. "Can you ride?" he asked.

"Good land!" Will exclaimed. "I learned to ride before I could walk."

Mr. Ewing agreed to give Will a job. When he learned that his new ranch hand had run away from school, he wrote to Will's father and told him where his son was employed. Clem answered promptly.

"You're welcome to keep Willie," he wrote. "If you can get any work out of him, it will be more than I was ever able to do."

Will turned out to be a good cowboy. He not only amused the men in the bunkhouse with his witty remarks and his roping tricks, but he also worked hard.

Soon Mr. Ewing decided to drive 600 head of cattle to market on foot. On the

long drive from Texas to Kansas, Will did his full share of the work, and he endured good-naturedly the discomforts of camping and taking care of cattle in rainy weather.

When the cattle drive ended, the other cowboys lined up to receive their pay, but Will did not.

"Here is your money, Will," said Mr. Ewing, when he had paid the other men. "Thirty dollars for your share of the work."

Will shuffled his feet and rubbed his chin in embarrassment. "Shucks, Mr. Ewing," he protested. "I couldn't rightly take money for that. Why, I just had myself a good time. A fellow can't take pay for having fun." He did accept pay for his regular work on the ranch, however.

After four months in Texas, Will grew restless. He gave up his job and returned home. The first thing he did was to repay his sisters the money they had sent him.

Uncle Clem had moved to Claremore, the big town in the district, to devote himself to banking and the politics of the Cherokee Nation.

"Willie," he said, "I'd like you to take over the supervision of the ranch."

"Oh, Papa!" Will protested. "I don't want to!"

For once Uncle Clem laid down the law to his son. "If you won't go to school, and you won't work, you won't get any more money from me."

The threat of no money didn't bother Will, but his father's disapproval did. For a few months he tried running the ranch, but he was bored. He had trouble sticking to the ordinary, everyday work of ranching. When he should have been branding calves, he was halfway across the Territory, competing in a roping contest. That was lots more fun than ranching.

4. "Itchy Foot"

In the fall of 1900 Will took a trip to Kansas City, Missouri. He learned some new songs, and he bought a banjo and shipped it home.

When Will got off the train at Oologah on his return, he went into the railroad station to claim his banjo. To his surprise, at the ticket window he saw a strange girl, and a pretty one at that.

"Can I help you?" she asked.

Will had a sudden attack of shyness.

He whirled and fled, without asking for his instrument.

Will soon learned that the new girl was Betty Blake. She had come from Arkansas for a long visit with her sister, whose husband was the Oologah station agent.

A few days later one of Will's friends gave a supper party and invited both Will Rogers and Betty Blake. Will was very quiet during the meal, but in the living room after supper he began to sing in his high tenor the new songs he had learned in Kansas City. He had to sing without accompaniment because he had not yet claimed his banjo.

Before the party was over, Will handed Betty his new sheet music. "If you'll learn to play these on your sister's piano," he suggested, "I'll get my banjo and we can play and sing some evening."

Will soon claimed his banjo, and he and Betty spent a happy evening together playing and singing. Before the evening was over, they were good friends.

Late in the fall Betty returned to Arkansas. Will wrote to her, but her replies were slow and rather cool. He soon stopped writing.

Uncle Clem, trying to get his son to settle down, offered him the profits from

Betty, second from right, and Will, at far left, with a wagonload of friends in 1900

a herd of cattle if he would care for them and market them.

The money Will made on that herd fairly burned a hole in his pocket. Instead of depositing the money in his father's bank or buying more cattle, Will had another idea.

"I'm going to South America, Papa," he announced one day. "Dick Parris is going with me."

"Why in the world do you want to go to South America?" Uncle Clem demanded.

"Oh, just to see the country," Will replied. "I understand they need cowboys down in Argentina."

"You've got an itchy foot," roared his father. "How much money has Dick Parris got?"

"None," Will answered blithely. "I'm going to pay his way."

Uncle Clem gave up trying to reason with his harum-scarum son. Early in 1902, Will and his cousin started on their long journey.

Will wrote from Argentina:

> Dear Papa:
> The work and cattle business here is nothing like it is at home. The head men leave most of the work to peons or natives, who get about $5 a month in our money and have to live like dogs....
> This is no place to make money unless you have at least ten thousand dollars to invest....You don't know how good your country is until you get away from it.

Will's money dwindled fast. Both of the boys became homesick, but Will had only enough money left for one steamship ticket to New York. He bought a ticket for his friend and he himself stayed on in South America.

During the next few months, Will seldom had a job. Sometimes he had to sleep in a park. He had only one dollar left when he was offered a job on a cattle boat headed for South Africa. He jumped at the chance to get away from Argentina.

For months Will wandered over South Africa. He saw vast sugar plantations, great cattle herds, diamond, gold, and coal mines, and natives wearing rings, chains, and scrap iron in their ears and noses. He worked at one job after another, always with horses, cattle, or mules. He became more homesick than ever, but he had no money for steamship fare. He was too proud to ask his father, and for the first time in Will's life, Uncle Clem did not offer any money.

34

One day early in 1903, in Johannesburg, a sign caught Will's eye: "Texas Jack's Wild West Show."

Will's heart leaped. That must be an American company! He hurried to find Texas Jack.

"I reckon I'm a neighbor of yours," Will said. "I'm from Indian Territory."

"Glad to meet you," said Texas Jack, a tall, lean man in colorful cowboy clothes.

"I'd like to join your outfit," Will told him.

The show owner studied Will for a moment. "Can you ride?" Will nodded eagerly. "Can you handle a rope?"

"Yes, sir," Will responded.

"Show me one of your tricks."

Will borrowed a rope from a member of the company. He decided to do the difficult "crinoline" trick. He coiled the rope

carefully, then started a small loop spinning. Gradually he played out the rope, and the loop grew larger and larger. When all the rope had been used up, Will had an immense loop spinning around him.

Texas Jack nodded gravely. "You'll do. You've got a job—twenty dollars a week." With that he walked away.

The owner of the rope came up to claim it. "Too bad, kid," he said.

"What's too bad?" Will inquired.

"You just passed up a chance to make two hundred and fifty dollars," the man replied.

"Good land!" Will exclaimed. "How?"

"Texas Jack has a standing offer of two hundred and fifty dollars to any outsider who can do the 'crinoline,'" the man explained. "Now that you're a member of the company you can't collect."

Will thought of all he could have done with two hundred and fifty dollars. He could have gone home to Indian Territory! Then he shrugged and said cheerfully, "No use crying over spilled milk."

Billed as the Cherokee Kid, Will played all over South Africa in Texas Jack's Wild West Show. He kept the money he earned in a money belt around his waist, so that one day he could prove to the folks at home that he had been a success in show business.

After a year Will grew restless again. He decided to see more of the world before going home, and he took passage on a ship for Australia. There he joined the Wirth Brothers Circus. Billed again as the Cherokee Kid, he toured Australia and New Zealand for eight months, and his money belt grew fuller and fuller.

One evening some circus people invited
Will to join them in a game of cards.

"No, thanks, fellows," Will replied. "I
never did rightly learn any gambling
games." He didn't drink or smoke either,
and he knew that at the gambling parties

there was a lot of drinking and smoking.

"Oh, come on," urged the others. "You can afford to risk a few dollars to learn how to play."

Will allowed himself to be persuaded. At first he won a little money, and then he began to lose. He lost every cent his money belt contained!

"I'll never gamble again," he vowed. And he never did.

Back at the circus, Will again started to save his money. When he had enough for steamship fare, he sailed for San Francisco, in April, 1904.

Will had been away for two years. He had traveled thousands of miles, seen many sights, and earned a considerable amount of money. Yet he had come home without a cent. He had to ride a freight train home.

5. "All My Feet But One"

The Louisiana Purchase Exposition had just opened in St. Louis, Missouri. An Indian Territory man, Colonel Zacharias Mulhall, had organized a Wild West show to play at the fair. He offered Will a job as rider and trick roper.

Will had just finished his act one day when a note signed "Betty Blake" was handed to him. Betty was in St. Louis visiting a sister and wanted to see him.

Will remembered the pretty girl in the Oologah railroad station. Quickly he sent her an answer: "Will you come to the show tomorrow and have dinner with me afterward?"

When Will dressed for his act the following afternoon, he put on a red velvet suit trimmed with yards of gold braid, that he had worn in his Australian circus act. It was an eye-catching outfit, Will thought, as he got dressed.

His costume was eye-catching indeed, so much so that it embarrassed Betty Blake. While Will went through his roping act, Betty's sister and her friend teased Betty about her fancy "Indian cowboy." When Will, dressed in his customary jeans, colored shirt, and bright bandanna joined the girls after the show, he sensed that Betty wished she hadn't come.

Will soon managed to get Betty away from the other girls, so that he could talk with her alone. When he learned that his gaudy, tight suit had been a source of embarrassment to Betty, he vowed never to wear it again. They had a happy evening together touring the fair, and when they parted at her sister's door they promised to write to each other.

The summer ended, and with it Colonel Mulhall's Wild West Show. Soon the colonel had an invitation to put on a riding and roping exhibition for the Horse Fair at New York's Madison Square Garden. Again he gave Will a job.

When the Horse Fair closed, Will remained in New York. He wanted to get a job in vaudeville, a type of variety show that was popular then. Will planned to rope a running horse on stage. He hired a rider, made felt carpet slippers for his horse Teddy, and then he practiced and

practiced with the horse and the rider until the act was perfect.

Will's first appearance was at the supper show at the Union Square Theater. In spite of his careful preparations and arduous hours of practicing, he was nervous when the time came to go on the stage. He popped a stick of chewing gum in his mouth to soothe his nerves, knocked on wood, and then shuffled out on the stage.

The day had been sweltering. Now, at 6:30 in the evening, the audience seemed half asleep. In silence Will began his act. One rope trick ... two ... three. The audience still drowsed. Then Will coiled his rope, made a new loop, and twirled it around his head.

Suddenly his horse Teddy raced out on the stage, with a rider on his back. Quick as a flash Will sent his loop flying. It caught Teddy smoothly and the horse stopped short.

The audience sat up straight, suddenly wide awake in spite of the heat. That was a trick worth watching!

Will practiced continually and kept improving his act. To his disappointment audiences didn't seem to appreciate his most difficult tricks. Will grumbled about this to his fellow actors.

"Your tricks look so easy," one actor pointed out. "You should announce the difficult ones."

At the next performance, before beginning his double-rope stunt, Will paused and walked to the front of the stage.

"Folks," he drawled, "I want to call your attention to my next trick—it's a double-roping act. I'm going to catch horse and rider at the very same time, with separate ropes." He hesitated and then added with a sheepish grin, "That is, I'll do it if I'm lucky, and I'm not sure I will be."

The audience roared with laughter, and Will was indignant. He hadn't meant to be funny. In embarrassed, angry silence he performed his trick. Then he stalked off the stage, vowing he would never again speak to an audience.

The older actor congratulated him. "That was great, Will," he said. "In show business you get every laugh you can."

So Will began to work for laughs. He took to commenting on his act as he worked with his ropes. Once, when he missed in trying to jump through a loop, he grinned at his audience and observed, "Well, I got all my feet through but one."

That remark drew such a big laugh that Will used it many times.

If his rope slipped off the horse in his double-roping act, Will would say ruefully, "I should have spread a little glue on his nose so the rope would stick."

Sometimes Will missed a throw deliberately, in order to joke about it. His audiences seemed to like his mistakes even more than his successes. More and more people came to see his act, and Will's pay was increased.

After seven months in New York and a European tour, Will went to see Betty.

"I love you," he said. "I've loved you for years. Won't you marry me?"

Betty loved Will, but in the small town where she grew up acting was not an approved profession. "If you were a rancher, Will," she said, "I'd marry you in a minute. But my folks don't want me to marry a showman."

Will had no intention of giving up his hard-won, successful stage career. As Uncle Clem often observed, "There's a lot of mule in Willie." So Betty and Will parted sadly. Will continued with his act and Betty tried to forget him.

Two years went by. Then Will showed up at the Blake house unannounced. He was on his way back to New York City after a visit to Claremore to see his father, who had been ill.

"Pack up your things, Blake," Will told Betty. "You're going back to New York with me."

"I am?" asked Betty weakly. "But you're still in show business."

"Sure," Will admitted.

Betty was now 28 and Will was 29. If they were ever going to marry, she knew, they shouldn't put it off much longer. "All right, Will," she said. "I'll marry you, no matter what my folks say."

"I'll leave the theater after this year," Will promised. "But you'll like show business, Blake, once you get used to it. After my New York engagement, we go on tour. You'll get to see a lot of the country."

They were married in Betty's home the day before Thanksgiving, 1908. After the wedding they boarded a train for New York City.

6. *Follies* Comedian

Betty and Will had a marvelous time together those first months in New York. Will loved showing his bride, who had never been much more than 200 miles from home, all the wonderful sights of the big city. When the show went on tour, Betty went along.

Will's "itchy foot" wouldn't let him rest. He wanted to be doing something all the time—working, sight-seeing, riding, or practicing roping. Sometimes Betty found it hard to keep up with him, but she loved him and she loved being with him.

Although Will earned good money, he hadn't saved any. He was always giving it away to people in need, especially cowboys, actors, and Indian Territory people. He could never refuse any request.

One day a hobo asked for money. "I was a rider with you in Mulhall's show," he said.

Will grinned. "You don't look like you was a rider," he said. "You look like you had been rode." But he gave the man some bills.

"We should start saving money, Will," Betty said. "We'll need something to live on when you retire from the stage."

Will agreed. He bought a big steel box with a slot in it, and every day he poked a dollar through the slot. While they were out West, where silver dollars were far more common than dollar bills, the box grew very heavy. The other show people teased Will about his "strongbox."

One winter day in Butte, Montana, after an afternoon of ice skating, Will and Betty returned to their hotel room. Betty let out an anguished shriek.

"Will! Our strongbox!"

On the floor, on top of Will's ropes, lay their battered steel box and a brand-new axe.

"Good land!" Will cried. "Our money is all gone!"

Betty sat down on the bed and cried, but Will tried to laugh off the loss. "What's half a year's savings, Blake? Easy come, easy go."

Still Betty wept. Will tried a few jokes, but they fell flat. At last he pulled his wife to her feet, and dried her eyes on his bandanna. "Come on now, honey. There's no use crying over spilled milk. Let's go out and get a good dinner."

Will and Betty started another retirement fund immediately, but they did not talk about it to others.

The tour continued. Betty grew tired of traveling and began to count the days until they would settle down.

Late in the spring Will got a good offer for an engagement the following year. Betty repeated the salary figure wonderingly.

"I suppose you can't afford to turn that down, can you?" she asked slowly. "Claremore will have to wait." So Will Rogers and his wife returned to New York City for another season.

The next year it was the same story... and the next... and the next. Claremore remained a dream.

All this time Will had kept his horse in the act, but he did more and more talking to his audiences.

"Swingin' a rope's all right," he remarked casually one night, "if your neck ain't in it." The audience howled with delight.

The theater manager said to Betty, "People pay lots more attention to Will and what he says than they do to his horse and his ropes. Why does he bother with the rest of his act?"

The following week Will sent his horse and rider home. But he kept his ropes, because he talked better when his hands were busy. From that time on he had a solo act, talking constantly while he performed rope tricks. To his audiences he explained, "I found out you folks want gags, not nags."

Will, on stage, attracted large audiences with
his rope tricks and his warm humor.

The busy, happy years passed rapidly. Will and Betty loved each other more and more. In 1911 their first child, Will, Jr., was born, and Betty was sure she was the luckiest woman in the world.

Will had now become a real success in the theater. At last Uncle Clem could be proud of his wayward son. But when he saw Will's act in New York Clem said wonderingly, "Why, Willie ain't acting! He's just being himself, acting the fool like always. And to think he gets paid for it!"

Indian Territory was now part of the new state of Oklahoma. Although Uncle Clem was growing frail, he remained active in Oklahoma politics. His home district, now called a county, was named Rogers in his honor. A few months later the old man died.

Will and Betty continued to make their home near New York. During the next few years two more children, Mary and James, were born to them. Another son, Freddie, born later, died in infancy of diphtheria.

One day Will told Betty, "The boss wants me to expand my act and do more talking."

"Good," said Betty. "You deserve more time."

"But what'll I jaw about?" Will asked. "I can't say the same things over and over."

"Why not talk about what you read in the papers?" Betty suggested. "You're always making funny remarks to me about what you read."

That night when Will went on stage he said, "All I know is what I read in the papers."

The audience roared. Will was surprised that they considered his introduction funny. Actually, his statement was true. He read half a dozen newspapers from front to back every day and was seldom seen without a rolled-up newspaper in his hand.

From then on Will used remarks about current events in his act. He had a knack for putting into words what people were thinking about national and international affairs.

In the spring of 1916 Florenz Ziegfeld offered Will a spot in his new show. For years Ziegfeld had been producing the *Follies*, a musical show featuring extravagant stage sets and beautiful girls in gorgeous costumes. Will wanted the job, because playing in the *Follies* was every comedian's dream. But Betty talked him out of it.

"When the New York run ends, the *Follies* will go on tour," she pointed out. "You'd have to leave the children and me for months." Reluctantly, Will refused Ziegfeld's offer.

Will and Betty went to the opening performance of the *Follies*. It was a colorful spectacle, but Will fidgeted in his seat. Soon he nudged his wife.

"What'd I tell you, Blake? This show needs something besides pretty girls."

A minute later he prodded her again. "I could've livened it up."

By the time the performance ended, Betty was sorry she had opposed Will about joining the *Follies*. However, a few days later Mr. Ziegfeld telephoned Will and again offered him the job. This time Will accepted. But he refused to sign a contract.

"Where I come from," he told Mr. Ziegfeld, "a man's word is all you need. Let's shake hands on our deal." And they did.

Will's act was a tremendous success. His performance "livened up" the *Follies of 1916.* The moment he ambled out on stage, grinning bashfully, rope in hand, hair in his eyes, jaws working hard on his wad of gum, the audience began to applaud.

7. "What I Read in the Papers"

Betty was very proud of Will's growing reputation, and she reconciled herself to the prospect of his long absence from New York when the show went on tour. Something annoyed her, however, and that was Will's dressing room at the theater.

Although Will was one of the stars of the *Follies*, his dressing room was a disgrace, Betty thought. A dingy cubbyhole with a crude makeshift shower, it had a row of hooks along the wall, a few kitchen chairs, and only a shelf for a dressing

The *Follies* girls and their favorite cowboy

table. There was no couch, or even an armchair. Once she found Will resting on the floor, his overcoat covering him.

Betty decided to surprise Will with a redecorated, refurnished dressing room. She sneaked in while he was onstage and measured and planned.

One evening when Will arrived at the theater, he thought he had gotten into the wrong dressing room. This one had a rug, a comfortable couch, some easy chairs, and a curtain at the tiny window.

As Will stood there staring, he heard a girlish giggle. Then Betty stepped out from behind the new shower curtain. "Like it, Will?" she asked.

Her pleasure faded quickly. It was obvious that her surprise did not please Will at all.

"Good land, Blake!" he protested. "I can't have my dressing room fancied up."

"But you ought to be comfortable," Betty insisted. "You didn't even have a place to lie down before."

"Sure I did," Will replied. "I just lay down on the floor." He began to shove the easy chairs out into the hall. Near tears, Betty watched as the couch and chairs were given away to other actors, and the curtain and rug banished from the room.

In 1918 Will Rogers began to appear in silent films. When he was offered a two-year contract, Will accepted but refused to read the contract. He still considered a handshake binding.

Will loved moviemaking. "It's the grandest show business in the world," he said. "A fellow can act, and then he can sit down and clap for himself."

He liked to finish a picture ahead of schedule, to have more time for roping and riding. But then he would remember how many days' pay the stagehands and electricians had lost, and he would pay them out of his own pocket.

Now that he was working in Hollywood, Will moved his family from New York to California. He purchased a home in Beverly Hills and later bought a ranch. But he was happiest in a rustic cabin.

The Rogers family at their Beverly Hills
home: Will Jr., Will, Jim, Betty, Mary

"You're just like an old full blood,"
chuckled his sister Maude. "You buy a big
house, then build a little cabin to live in."

Now that there was room for horses,
daily riding became a part of the Rogers'
family life. Even Jimmy, the smallest

child, rode. Almost every day Will practiced rope tricks and roping, using calves he kept in a corral at the ranch for the purpose. Soon the calves learned that Will's roping wouldn't hurt them, and instead of running away, they would trot up to him. Then Will bought new calves.

Will had one calf, however, that never had to be replaced, a stuffed calf on rollers. When friends dropped in, Will got

out his stuffed calf and his ropes, and put on a roping exhibition in the Rogers' high-ceilinged living room.

Will had often been urged to write articles and books, but when he tried to be funny in his writing, he wasn't.

"You're only funny when you're being yourself," Betty told him. So he stopped trying to make his writing humorous. He simply wrote as he talked, and editors

and readers liked it. This was one of his comments:

America and England are regular old busybodies when it comes to telling somebody else what to do. We are going to get a kick in the pants some day if we don't... start tending to our own business and let other people live as they want to.

When he was criticized for using "ain't" in his writing, Will replied:

Maybe ain't ain't so correct, but I notice that lots of folks who ain't using ain't, ain't eating.

Will Rogers was now writing a weekly article on current events. It appeared in many Sunday papers, including *The New York Times.*

8. Crony of Kings

In his stage act and in his articles, Will continually "kidded the public." He especially liked to poke fun at prominent people. He wrote:

> When I die my epitaph is going to read, "I joked about every prominent man of my time, but I never met a man I didn't like."

When Will Rogers was introduced to the president of the United States, he stuck out his hand and said, "Mighty pleased to meet you, but I didn't catch the name." Sober President Coolidge couldn't help smiling.

One day in 1925 Will received a letter, supposedly from a lecture manager, offering to arrange a lecture tour. "I will pay your traveling expenses," the writer stated, "and guarantee six lectures a week at one thousand dollars a night." The signature read, "Charles L. Wagner."

Will tossed the letter into the wastebasket. Somebody's idea of a joke, he thought. Weeks later Mr. Wagner telephoned him, and Will learned that the offer was not a joke.

"Shucks, Mr. Wagner," Will said, "I just couldn't do it. I talk to folks, sure. But I'm no lecturer."

Wagner persuaded him to give it a try. To Will's amazement his lectures were enormously popular, and he loved the work. On his first tour he spoke 151 times, always fitting his remarks to his audience. Talking to a group of aristocratic Boston women, Will drawled, "My ancestors didn't come over on the Mayflower like yours. They met the boat."

When Will arrived in a new town, he always went first to a newspaper office. There he asked questions about the town, the police, the traffic, and so on.

"Who's the richest man in town?" he would ask. "What's going on in the schools? What kind of a mayor have you got?"

When he went on stage that evening, chewing gum, Will talked first about local affairs, mentioning names freely. He "kidded" the mayor, the city council, and the town's most prominent people. Then he turned to national and international

events, joking about politics and world problems.

"Our foreign dealings are an open book," he observed one night, "generally a checkbook."

"You're doing fine," he told the audience when they laughed. "We'll get out early tonight. It takes twice as long to finish when you have to explain the jokes."

Onstage, Will never stood still. He walked up and down, jingling the coins in his pocket. He leaned against the piano, or sat on the piano stool. Sometimes he wandered downstage and sat on the edge of the platform with his legs dangling over it. The crowd loved him. Finally he brought out his ropes and began to spin them, still talking. About midnight he would say, "You folks go home. I'm tired of messing with you."

Even after he was a celebrity, Will found time to practice roping.

When the lecture tour ended in mid-April, 1926, Will decided to go to Europe, taking his son Bill with him. He wanted to gather material for a series of magazine articles to be called, "Letters of a Self-made Diplomat to his President."

Before sailing, Will dropped in at *The New York Times*, which published his weekly articles. As he was leaving, Adolph Ochs, the publisher, said, "If you run across anything worthwhile in Europe, Will, cable it to us. We'll pay the tolls."

Will and Bill had a wonderful time in Europe, flying wherever they went.

In spite of several accidents, Will had been an aviation fan ever since his first flight in 1915. "Airplanes are going to give trains and buses a run for their money," he predicted. "Pretty soon folks are going to fly everywhere."

Wiley Post, a fellow Oklahoman, was one of Will's favorite pilots. Years before, Wiley had lost an eye. Will wrote about his friend:

> The eye he lost saw the bad weather and bad landing fields, the good one just saw the good ones. When Wiley Post says quit, you can bet there's no more gas or no more air.

In June, Betty and the other children met Will in London, and the family toured England. Then Will insisted that he and Betty fly to Holland.

It was Betty's first flight and she was stiff with fright. As the ground dropped away from under the little plane, she clutched her husband's arm.

Will laughed. "Woman, don't hold onto me. I couldn't help you any. I sorta wish, myself, there was a fire brigade under us with a net."

The plane landed safely. Will was eager to go up again, but Betty preferred land travel.

"Promise me, Will," she said "you'll never become a pilot." Will promised.

Will Rogers accomplished a lot that summer in Europe. He made a movie in England, appeared in six travelogue films, acted in a musical show, gave radio talks, and wrote his weekly articles for the Sunday papers in the United States.

He made friends with kings, princes, and statesmen. When he met the Prince of Wales, a fellow polo player, he said, "Howdy, Prince. How're you fallin'?" Will met other interesting people, too—actors, writers, cab drivers, charwomen, waiters, and sales clerks.

One July afternoon Will and Betty had
lunch with Lady Astor, an American
heiress who had married an Englishman
and was now a member of Parliament.
The next day Will sent a cable to Adolph
Ochs in New York:

> Nancy Astor, which is the *nom
> de plume* of Lady Astor, is arriv-
> ing on your side about now. She is
> the best friend America has here.
> Please ask my friend Jimmy
> Walker [Mayor of New York] to
> have New York take good care of
> her. She is the only one here that
> don't throw rocks at American
> tourists.
>
> Will Rogers

Mr. Ochs printed the cable in a prominent spot in *The New York Times* and
cabled Will a request for more such material. Will hastened to oblige.

A woman had just swum the English Channel, and Will wrote:

I wanted my wife to try it, but the Channel is all booked up for the next month.

Later he observed:

England has the greatest statesmen and the poorest coffee in the world.

Will wrote his comments on trains, ships, and in his cheerfully cluttered study.

About a British Parliament session he wrote:

> A man who was engaged for that business prayed. He mentioned the King more than he did the subjects. . . . I thought the subjects should have an even break.

Back in the United States that fall, Will began to write a newspaper paragraph every day. Often he began it with, "All I know is what I read in the papers." Eventually, 400 papers carried his daily comments.

9. "Will Rogers Says..."

Will's vaudeville act, his lectures, and especially his newspaper articles, had made him famous. Millions of people turned first to the "box" containing "Will Rogers Says..." when they opened their morning papers. A reporter observed, "His droll comments on men and events have become so popular that he finds himself—probably to his surprise—a national figure."

Will made a great many goodwill trips abroad, visiting nearly every country in the world. He became almost as well known abroad as he was at home.

About his trip to Russia Will wrote:

They seem to keep on living—
but in all the time I was in Russia
I never saw anyone smile.

Everywhere Will went people recognized him. If he paused on a street corner to buy a newspaper or entered a restaurant for some chili, somebody spotted him and a crowd would gather. Hordes of tourists drove past his ranch, hoping to catch a glimpse of him.

In December 1926, Will Rogers returned to Beverly Hills to find a great crowd and a brass band waiting to welcome him back home.

"You have been elected the mayor of Beverly Hills," the spokesman told Will, presenting him with an immense scroll five feet long.

This was really a joke because Beverly Hills had no mayor. Will accepted the honor with a grin and a quip. "I'm for the common people," he said. "Since Beverly Hills has no common people, I'll be sure to make good."

Will boasted later, "I'm the only mayor that never made a mistake. I never made a decision."

The Cherokee Nation gave him the title of "Honorary Chief," and that was not a joke.

Soon after Will resumed his lecture tour, the Mississippi River flooded its banks and drove thousands of people from their homes. At once Will canceled his lecture engagements and went on tour for the Red Cross. At each benefit performance he started the pledges rolling with a substantial donation of his own. He raised $100,000 for the flood victims. For many years he gave one-tenth of his earnings to the Red Cross, besides contributing generously to many other charities.

When the 1928 presidential campaign got under way, people began to say that Will Rogers would make a good president.

Will laughed at the idea. He also laughed off requests to run for governor of Oklahoma, United States senator, and ambassador to Mexico.

"Can't," he said. "I look terrible in a dress suit."

In the 1932 presidential campaign, Will was again mentioned as a candidate. This time, at the Democratic National Convention, Oklahoma's 22 votes were cast for

Will Rogers. Will, who attended political conventions to "keep an eye on the government," was sitting in the press box. But reporters noticed that he slept through his nomination for the highest office in the land!

"Politics ain't on the level," Will complained next day in his newspaper paragraph. "I was in 'em for an hour, but in that short time somebody stole 22 votes from me."

When sound was added to motion pictures, 20th Century-Fox put Will Rogers under contract to make three movies a year. Some of his sound pictures, *A Connecticut Yankee in King Arthur's Court*, *State Fair*, *Lightnin',* and *David Harum*, became big hits.

Unlike Will's shabby dressing room at the *Follies*, his dressing room on the Fox

Will became even better known in movies like *Life Begins at Forty*, right, and *State Fair*, below.

lot was a well-furnished bungalow but Will seldom used it. He much preferred to sit in his cluttered old car while waiting to be called for a scene. He would curl up on the front seat and "snooze," or lift out his portable typewriter from the litter in the back seat and write his daily feature, "Will Rogers Says..."

With the typewriter propped on his knees, Will pecked out his paragraph in capital letters, using one finger of each hand. He never allowed an editor to change a word of what he wrote, not even the spelling or punctuation. Still, he never seemed to realize fully the influence that his homely, irreverent remarks had on his readers at home and abroad.

"Why do people call me a philosopher?" he wondered. "That's a fellow who studies things out. I don't even study 'em in."

10. The Final Flight

In the early summer of 1935 Will was working on his nineteenth talking movie, *Steamboat 'Round the Bend*. For the first time in his life, at 55, he complained of being tired, and his "Injun eyes" had begun to bother him. Will refused to see an eye doctor, however. He liked a friend's glasses so he bought half a dozen pairs at a time, and insisted that they fit him perfectly. He always wore them on the end of his nose.

One day Will announced to Betty, "Wiley

Post is in town, Blake. He wants me to fly to Alaska with him." Will considered Wiley, who had made two round-the-world flights, the best pilot he had ever met.

Betty started to say, "Please don't go, Will." Then she stopped.

It had taken Betty Rogers years to learn that she could not change Will in any way. She had not been able to persuade him to accept comfort in his *Follies* dressing room. She had never convinced him that he should dress up for certain special occasions, instead of wearing a worn blue serge suit. Her pleas to Will to be careful of his health and safety fell on deaf ears. Although Will adored her, she had been the one throughout their long, happy marriage to change and adjust. She had done it willingly because he meant so much to her.

Now Betty knew that Will wanted her to be happy about his plans, so she smiled cheerfully and said, "When will you start?"

On August 5, 1935, after attending a rodeo, Betty and Will drove to the airport, and Betty saw him off on the 11 P.M. plane. He was going to meet Wiley in Seattle. There, they loaded the little seaplane—not forgetting two cases of chili for Will—and then took off for Alaska.

Juneau . . . Anchorage . . . Matanuska . . . Fairbanks—everywhere they put down, Will found old friends or made new ones. At each stop he sent off his daily telegram to the newspapers.

In Fairbanks the weather turned bad. Fog closed in. Barrow, where Will had a friend, was to be the next stop. It was 327 miles north of the Arctic Circle, on the other side of a rugged range of high mountains. Each day the fliers radioed to Barrow for the weather report, and each day it came back: Fog.

Will and Wiley grew restless. Finally Wiley said, "I think we can make it."

Will grinned. "If it's good enough for you, it's good enough for me."

The fliers took off from Fairbanks at about 11 A.M. on August 15. Wiley Post, expert aviator that he was, piloted the little plane safely over the wild mountains in spite of the dense fog. Then he headed east for Barrow.

The fog was like cotton batting. The fliers could see nothing below. Yet Wiley Post felt that Barrow should be directly underneath. Three times he sent the plane in a great circle. On the third round Will Rogers shouted, "Look! Water! A tent!"

Through a rift in the fog Wiley saw a lagoon big enough to put his seaplane down. When they had landed, both men walked out on the pontoons and surveyed the situation. The water in this lagoon was only a few feet deep. The ground around it was still frozen.

An Eskimo couple came to the edge of the water from their nearby camp.

"Where are we?" Will called to them. "Is this Barrow?"

The man did not understand, but his wife knew a little English. "Not Barrow," she replied. "Barrow over there." She pointed in the opposite direction from the way the plane was headed.

"What are you fishing for?" Will asked, observing a tent and fishing gear.

"For seals," the woman answered, returning Will's sunny smile.

Will Rogers and Wiley Post waved their thanks to the Eskimos and got back in the cockpit. Wiley took off, then turned the plane toward Barrow. After being lost in the fog, he was dangerously low on gas.

Suddenly the engine misfired. Something was wrong. The little plane plummeted back into the shallow lagoon. It landed upside down with such force that the plane split open. Sand, gravel, and water sprayed high into the air and inside the broken airplane. The Eskimo man ran into the lagoon and shouted. There was no answer. Both Will Rogers and Wiley Post had died instantly.

When the news of Will Rogers' death was broadcast by radio, people all over the world mourned as if they had lost their best friend. The enormous flood of tributes and memorials would have surprised Will.

"Shucks," he once said. "I'm just an old cowhand that had a little luck. Why all this here fuss about me?"

Will's statue was placed in Statuary Hall of the Capitol Building in Washington, D.C. He himself had selected the spot jokingly, "so he could keep an eye on Congress."